# SPIDER-MAN 3

**Based on the screenplay by
Sam Raimi & Ivan Raimi
and Alvin Sargent**

**Screen Story by
Sam Raimi & Ivan Raimi**

**Based on the Marvel Comic Book
by Stan Lee and Steve Ditko**

LEVEL 3

**MSCHOLASTIC**

**Adapted by:** Helen Parker

**Fact Files written by:** Jane Rollason

**Publisher:** Jacquie Bloese

**Commissioning Editor:** Helen Parker

**Editor:** Jane Rollason

**Cover layout:** Emily Spencer

**Designer:** Victoria Wren

**Picture research:** Emma Bree

**Photo credits: Pages 56 & 57:** Allstar/Cinetext; M. Mainz, C. Gordon/Getty Images; Columbia Pictures/Marvel/Tribeca Film Festival. **Pages 60 & 61:** F. M. Frances, C. Ballentine, J. Fox/Alamy; R. Holmes/Corbis.

COLUMBIA PICTURES PRESENTS A MARVEL STUDIOS/LAURA ZISKIN PRODUCTION TOBEY MAGUIRE "SPIDER-MAN 3" KIRSTEN DUNST JAMES FRANCO THOMAS HADEN CHURCH TOPHER GRACE BRYCE DALLAS HOWARD ORIGINAL MUSIC THEMES BY DANNY ELFMAN SCORE BY CHRISTOPHER YOUNG EXECUTIVE PRODUCERS STAN LEE KEVIN FEIGE JOSEPH M. CARACCIOLO BASED ON THE MARVEL COMIC BOOK BY STAN LEE AND STEVE DITKO SCREEN STORY BY SAM RAIMI & IVAN RAIMI COLUMBIA PICTURES MARVEL SPIDER-MAN CHARACTER TM & © 2007 MARVEL CHARACTERS, INC. ALL RIGHTS RESERVED. SCREENPLAY BY SAM RAIMI & IVAN RAIMI AND ALVIN SARGENT PRODUCED BY LAURA ZISKIN AVI ARAD GRANT CURTIS DIRECTED BY SAM RAIMI SONY

sony.com/Spider-Man

Spider-Man and all related characters: ™ & © 2007 Marvel Characters, Inc. All rights reserved.

*Spider-Man 3*, the movie: © 2007 Columbia Pictures Industries, Inc. All rights reserved.

Published by Scholastic Ltd 2007

No part of this publication may be reproduced in whole or in part, or stored in a retrieval system, or transmitted in any form or by any means, electronic, mechanical, photocopying, recording or otherwise, without written permission of the publisher. For information regarding permission write to:
Mary Glasgow Magazines (Scholastic Ltd)
Euston House
24 Eversholt Street
London
NW1 1DB

Printed in Singapore. Reprinted in 2010.
This edition printed in 2011.

# CONTENTS

| | PAGE |
|---|---|
| **Spider-Man 3** | **4–55** |
| **People and places** | **4** |
| **Chapter 1:** 'Manhattan Memories' | **6** |
| **Chapter 2:** The Goblin returns | **10** |
| **Chapter 3:** Sandman | **15** |
| **Chapter 4:** Lost memories | **20** |
| **Chapter 5:** The key and the kiss | **24** |
| **Chapter 6:** A painful evening | **28** |
| **Chapter 7:** A new Spider-Man | **32** |
| **Chapter 8:** Washed away | **35** |
| **Chapter 9:** Revenge | **41** |
| **Chapter 10:** The Jazz Room | **46** |
| **Chapter 11:** Partners in crime | **51** |
| **Epilogue:** The songbird | **55** |
| **Fact Files** | **56–61** |
| *Spider-Man 3* – the film | **56** |
| Spider-Man's enemies | **58** |
| Broadway – the street of dreams | **60** |
| **Self-Study Activities** | **62–64** |

## PEOPLE AND PLACES

# SPIDER

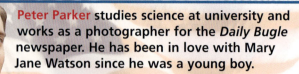

**Peter Parker** studies science at university and works as a photographer for the *Daily Bugle* newspaper. He has been in love with Mary Jane Watson since he was a young boy.

Peter is also **Spider-Man**. He uses his very special powers to stop crimes and save people's lives. He is New York City's own hero.

**Harry Osborn** was Peter Parker's best friend. He knows that Peter is Spider-Man. He thinks that Spider-Man killed his father, Norman Osborn, and he can't forgive Peter.

**Mary Jane Watson** (MJ) is an actress on Broadway. She grew up next door to Peter Parker. She loves Peter and knows that he is Spider-Man.

**Aunt May** is like a mother to Peter. Her husband, Uncle Ben, was murdered two years ago by a New York criminal. She lives alone and misses her husband very much.

# MAN 3

**Flint Marko** has escaped from prison. He will do anything to save his sick young daughter.

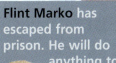

**Gwen Stacy** studies science at university with Peter and works as a model.

**Eddie Brock** is another photographer for the *Daily Bugle*. He thinks Gwen Stacy is his girlfriend.

**Venom** is fast and strong, and can fire webs like Spider-Man.

**The New Goblin** flies through New York City on his Sky-Stick.

## PLACES

**Manhattan** is the centre of New York City. All the biggest shops, tallest buildings and most famous places are here.
**Times Square** is on 42nd Street in the centre of Manhattan. It's famous for its signs in brightly coloured lights.
**Broadway** is a street in Manhattan where there are lots of theatres.
**The Jazz Room** is a music club in Manhattan.

**Sandman** can move like a sandstorm and is very strong.

## Chapter 1
## 'Manhattan Memories'

It was early evening in New York City. People were going to the theatre. They hurried past the bright lights of Times Square to Broadway. Peter Parker smiled to himself as he walked through the crowds. He was going to the theatre that evening, too. Suddenly, a group of little boys ran in front of him. They stopped and looked up at one of the signs. It said in lights, 'NEW YORK LOVES SPIDER-MAN!'

For the first time in his life Peter felt popular. Well, at least Spider-Man was popular. All the kids in the city wanted to be like Spider-Man. After all, he was a hero. The people of New York were safe when he was around. Uncle Ben would be so proud of him.

Peter's heart ached when he thought of his uncle. Uncle Ben was murdered two years ago, but for Peter the memory was still very fresh. Peter remembered the words Uncle Ben used to say: 'With great power comes great responsibility.' Peter had accepted his responsibility as Spider-Man and he felt good about that.

Peter Parker's life was so much better these days. He still didn't make much money as a photographer for the *Daily Bugle*. And he still lived in the same horrible little room. But some things *had* changed. As well as fighting crime, he was going to the university every day and he was now the best student in his class.

But best of all, Peter had Mary Jane Watson. He had always loved Mary Jane, or MJ as everyone called her. And tonight was her opening night on Broadway in 'Manhattan Memories'. As Peter stood outside the theatre he couldn't believe his luck – he finally had the girl.

He went inside. He was so proud that his girlfriend was the star of the show. Yes, everything was perfect … or almost perfect. The only thing missing was Harry Osborn.

Harry and Peter had been best friends since high school. But everything changed when Harry's father went crazy and became the Green Goblin. The Green Goblin had attacked New York and died in a fight with Spider-Man. Then Harry found out that Peter was Spider-Man. He couldn't forgive him for killing his father.

As Peter found his seat in the dark theatre, the musicians started to play. And then Mary Jane appeared. Peter was so excited. She looked amazing. When she started to sing, he felt she was singing just for him. Peter had never been so happy.

Harry was there, too. He watched Peter from his private box at the side of the theatre. He wasn't smiling.

'She was great,' thought Peter after the show. Maybe other people hadn't cheered as loudly as him. And maybe Peter was the only one standing up and cheering at the end. No, that didn't matter – she was great!

Suddenly, Peter saw a face he knew outside the theatre – it was Harry Osborn! Peter had tried several times to visit Harry at the offices of OsCorp*. Harry had refused to see him each time. Peter wanted to tell Harry that Norman Osborn's death was an accident.

'Harry!' Peter called as his friend got into a big expensive car. 'Harry, wait! You need to hear the truth.'

Harry turned to look at Peter. For a moment his heart told him he should listen to Peter this time. But a second later, the face of Norman Osborn seemed to appear at the window. 'Don't be weak!' Norman cried to his son.

Harry made a sign to his driver. Without a word, they drove away.

'Was I good?' asked Mary Jane as she put her arms around Peter later that evening.

'Good?' Peter smiled. 'You were great.'

Mary Jane went a little pink. Then she took Peter's hand and led him into her dressing room.

'I got your flowers,' she said warmly. 'Thank you. They're beautiful.' Then she pointed at a much bigger arrangement of flowers. 'And these are from Harry,' she said. 'Was he here tonight?'

Peter shook his head sadly. 'I saw him but he wouldn't talk to me.'

'I'm so sorry,' said MJ softly. 'What is it with you guys?'

'It's difficult,' said Peter. Although Mary Jane knew that Peter was Spider-Man, she didn't know exactly how Norman Osborn had died.

*The Osborn Corporation, a big scientific company started by Harry's father, Norman Osborn.*

The wind blew through Mary Jane's long red hair as they rode out of Manhattan on Peter's motorbike. It was wonderful to get out of the city for a little while.

Soon they found a good place to stop. Peter made a big web between two trees. They lay together in the web and looked up at the stars. High above them a shower of meteorites lit up the dark sky. It was a beautiful sight.

'Tell me you love me,' said MJ, looking into Peter's eyes. 'I like to hear it. It makes me feel safe.'

'I will always love you,' said Peter. 'I always have.'

Not far away from them, a small black rock hit the ground. But they didn't notice.

The rock was a meteorite. It was still hot after crashing down to Earth. Smoke rose from the rock and then something black and sticky came out of it. Something alive! It started to move across the grass like a spider. It jumped onto the back of Peter's motorbike. It hid there and waited …

# Chapter 2
## The Goblin returns

Flint Marko ran through the streets wearing his prison clothes. He knew the police were searching for him after his escape. He had to move quickly. He started to climb up the side of a building. Through a window, he saw a young girl asleep. He opened the window softly and climbed into her room. He took some letters from his pocket and put them very carefully next to the girl. Flint wrote these letters to her when he was in prison. The girl was his daughter, Penny. But she hadn't received them. His wife, Emma, had returned them all to him.

Silently, Flint went into his old bedroom and changed his clothes. He felt hungry and found some bread in the kitchen. A moment later Emma appeared. 'Get out of here!' she shouted. 'You're a bad man, Marko!'

They both knew that Penny was sick – very sick. Neither of them had enough money to pay her hospital bills. They didn't have much money before Flint went to prison. They had even less now.

Suddenly, Penny appeared and looked at her father with big eyes. She gave him her locket. He looked down at the silver heart in his hand. Even though he did bad things, Penny still loved her father.

'Get out!' his wife shouted. 'You're as useless as a grain of sand.'

'I'm not a bad person. I just had bad luck,' he said. 'I want to help you, Penny. That's the truth.'

Then he turned and jumped out of the window.

There was a knock on Aunt May's front door. She answered it and found Peter standing there. His eyes were shining and he had a big smile on his face.

'I'm going to ask Mary Jane to marry me,' he said.

Aunt May was excited and surprised – she wasn't expecting this.

'Let's have a cup of tea,' she said.

They sat down together in the kitchen. Aunt May remembered when Uncle Ben asked her to marry him. 'We were both frightened and excited, and very young,' she said.

'And you said "yes",' said Peter. 'Right?'

'No,' she said slowly. 'I wasn't ready. Love isn't enough, Peter. There's more to think about. You need a full-time job.'

Aunt May was right. If they wanted to start a family, he would need to earn more money. He could hardly pay for his room. A ring for Mary Jane was impossible.

Aunt May knew what Peter was thinking. She took off her diamond ring and put it in his hand.

'Think about how you're going to ask her, Peter,' she said. 'Make it special.'

Peter smiled. He had thought about that a lot. He knew just what he wanted to say. All he needed now was a better job. The *Daily Bugle* was looking for a full-time photographer. He was the only person who took photos of Spider-Man. 'Will they give me the job?' he wondered.

In a secret room in Harry Osborn's house, Harry stood behind glass walls. A special gas started to fill the air around him. Harry breathed in the gas through his mouth and his nose. Then he opened the glass doors and stepped out. He felt like a new man. He was stronger, faster and more powerful. He became the New Goblin.

'Now I'll be able to attack Spider-Man,' he thought. 'I'll get revenge for my father's death. My father will be proud of me!'

Peter waited nervously to speak to Jonah Jameson, or JJ as everyone called him, the boss at the *Daily Bugle*. He could hear him shouting in his office. He was often angry these days because sales were bad. People weren't buying enough copies of the newspaper. There weren't many crimes or exciting stories in New York City these days. And it was all Spider-Man's fault.

Just then another photographer, Eddie Brock, went into JJ's office. Suddenly, Peter realised that Eddie probably wanted the full-time job, too. Peter heard Eddie ask for more money. JJ hated talking about money. When it was finally Peter's turn to speak to JJ, he went crazy.

'You're not the only photographer in town!' he shouted.

Peter hurried out of JJ's office. 'I'll just have to try again later,' he thought.

Peter was riding his motorbike through the streets. Suddenly, something crashed into him. It was the Goblin! They both shot high into the sky on the Goblin's Sky-Stick*.

'But it can't be the Goblin!' thought Peter. He knew the Green Goblin was dead.

The New Goblin held onto Peter tightly. He pulled back Peter's head to show his throat. Knives shot out from the New Goblin's armour.

'Now I will get my revenge,' thought the Goblin.

Peter pulled away from the Goblin and fired a web at him. The New Goblin cut through the web but Peter managed to hold onto the side of a building. He looked down and saw the New Goblin on the Sky-Stick. The New Goblin pulled off his mask. Peter couldn't believe what he saw.

* *The New Goblin's flying machine.*

'Harry?' Peter said, amazed.
'Yes, Peter,' Harry replied. 'You knew this was coming!'
'I didn't kill your father,' Peter cried.
'Shut up!' Harry shouted as he fired a bomb at Peter. BOOM! Peter jumped quickly out of the way. Then he moved like a spider from building to building. He looked behind him; the New Goblin was getting closer. He fired a line of webbing between two buildings. Harry hit the webbing at full speed. He fell screaming from the Sky-Stick into the street below.

Harry was very badly hurt and Peter hurried to his side. He lifted Harry and carried him in his arms to hospital.

# Chapter 3
## Sandman

Flint Marko ran through some fields outside the city of New York. The police were close behind him now. He looked back and almost crashed into a wall. He didn't see the sign that read, 'DANGER! SCIENTIFIC TESTING. KEEP OUT!' He climbed over the wall and fell into a huge bowl of sand. He lay there waiting. He looked at the locket his daughter had given him. His heart ached for her. He had to try to escape …

Very slowly he got up. He looked around him and saw some strange guns pointing at him. Suddenly, with a terrible noise the guns fired at Flint. He screamed in pain as hot grains of sand hit his body. The grains burned whitehot and then Flint's whole body was turned to sand.

He tried to stand up and walk. He looked down at his body and almost cried. 'Look what they did to me. I'm not a man any more. I'm Sandman!' he thought. Then he saw something in the sand. It was Penny's locket!

'I must get it!' he thought.

Slowly, he managed to stand up and put one foot in front of the other. He reached down and picked up the locket.

'It doesn't matter that I'm made of sand,' he said to himself. 'I'm going to save my little girl. Nothing can stop me now.'

The next morning there was a knock on Peter's door. It was Mary Jane. She held up a newspaper.

Peter looked at the front page, but it wasn't about Spider-Man. 'Why are you showing me this?' he asked.

'Read the review,' said Mary Jane. 'They hated me.'

Peter couldn't believe it. 'But you were great,' he said.

Mary Jane turned to the reviews page and started to read. 'Young Miss Watson is a pretty girl. Easy on the eyes but not on the ears.'

'Spider-Man is attacked all the time in the papers,' said Peter.

'This isn't about you!' Mary Jane shouted. 'Try to understand how I feel!'

But at that moment there was an urgent report on Peter's police radio. A crane was about to crash into a building. People were in danger! They needed Spider-Man.

Peter looked at Mary Jane. She seemed so sad. She needed him. But Peter didn't really have a choice. He had to go. He just hoped that Mary Jane could understand.

Gwen Stacy stood in front of the camera and tried to smile. She was a university student, but she sometimes worked as a model to pay the bills. It was a very boring job today for office copiers. 'Why do they even need people in these photos?' Gwen wondered.

But the photographer wasn't looking at Gwen – he was looking through the window behind her. A huge crane had suddenly appeared right in the middle of his photograph!

'What's that thing doing in my background?' he said.

It started to move closer. A long, heavy piece of metal was hanging from the crane. And now it was swinging dangerously close to them …

'Get down!' Gwen shouted as the metal crashed through the window. Glass flew around them. Then the crane crashed into the building. Gwen screamed as the floor dropped away. She just managed to hold on and swung high above the ground. But then she couldn't hold on any longer … she screamed and fell … right into the arms of Spider-Man! She held onto him tightly.

'Boy, am I happy to see you!' she thought.

Down in the street below, Eddie Brock was taking photos of Spider-Man rescuing the girl.

'My God,' Eddie said to himself, 'that's Gwen ... that's my girl!'

Brock continued taking pictures as Spider-Man put Gwen safely on the ground.

'Beautiful,' Eddie said. 'Wait till you see the pictures, Gwen. Er ... Are you OK?'

Gwen managed a weak smile. 'I'm fine, Eddie.'

She didn't think of Eddie as her boyfriend. They had only been on one date. But Eddie felt differently. It made Gwen uncomfortable.

Eddie introduced himself to Spider-Man. 'I'm new,' he explained. 'I'm taking pictures of you for the *Daily Bugle* from now on.'

Later that day Eddie took his photo of Spider-Man and Gwen to Jonah Jameson at the *Daily Bugle*. JJ loved it. He was about to pay Eddie when Peter hurried into the office with his own photo of Spider-Man. Both shots were good, but JJ decided that Eddie's was better.

Perhaps Brock's photo was better this time, but Peter really wanted that full-time job. He had earned it. He needed it so he could marry MJ. The problem was that Eddie wanted it, too.

Jonah Jameson didn't care who got the job. He only cared about selling newspapers. He told them, 'I want a photo of Spider-Man doing something criminal. Then people will see that he really is a fake. The guy who brings me that photo gets the job.'

# Chapter 4
## Lost memories

Peter held the door open. Harry came slowly into the hall of his amazing home. He looked around as if he was a stranger. He couldn't remember much about anything.

'Thank God you're all right, sir,' said Bernard when he saw Harry. Bernard had worked for the Osborn family for many years. Harry remembered Bernard, but he didn't remember that he, Harry, was the New Goblin. Or that his best friend, Peter, was Spider-Man.

Peter was so happy to have his old friend back. He had brought him a present.

'It's your old basketball,' said Harry. 'Thanks!'

Harry threw the ball a couple of times against the floor, then shot the ball at Peter.

'It looks like money isn't a problem,' Harry said, looking around the place.

Peter laughed as he caught the ball. 'Harry, you're super rich!'

Slowly, Harry walked towards a painting of his father, Norman Osborn.

'I can't remember much about him. I'd really like to know more.'

'He loved you. That's the most important thing,' Peter replied, feeling uneasy. He threw the ball back to Harry, but he threw it too hard. Harry moved with amazing speed. He caught the ball before it broke anything expensive. Harry looked at Peter with surprise on his face.

'Did you see that?' asked Harry.

Peter tried to act cool. 'You were always a fast mover,' he said and smiled.

'Don't let one bad review stop you,' Mary Jane told herself as she walked to work the next day. She tried to walk proudly into the theatre. She pushed open the heavy door and was surprised to hear someone singing *her* song. Suddenly, the music stopped and everyone turned to look at MJ. For a moment nobody spoke.

The director turned to his assistant. 'Didn't anybody call her?' he whispered.

MJ's heart stopped.

'You dropped me after one bad review?' she said.

The producer stepped forward and said coldly, 'All the reviews were bad.'

Mary Jane could hardly breathe. Fighting back the tears, she turned and ran out of the theatre.

It was a very special day for Peter. The city of New York was giving Spider-Man the key to the city. Peter thought about all the bad stories the *Daily Bugle* had printed about Spider-Man. For a long time the people of New York thought Spider-Man was a criminal. But over the years, he had saved many lives. And now everyone knew he was a hero – everyone except Jonah Jameson.

A big crowd of people had come to see Spider-Man. Peter looked at all the excited faces. Just then Peter saw Mary Jane. He pushed through the crowd to reach her. He smiled at her excitedly. He didn't ask why she wasn't at the theatre. MJ really wanted to tell him. But this was his moment. 'I'm proud of you,' she said.

Peter pointed to a tall building at the corner of the square. 'I'm going to swing in from there.'

'Give them a good show,' Mary Jane replied.

'You, too,' Peter said with a smile. 'And don't worry about that review. We'll laugh about it tomorrow.'

Flint Marko was back in Manhattan. He was walking down a street when some police officers saw him. He hid behind a truck. The officers ran to the truck, but Marko had disappeared. They looked under the truck but he wasn't there. Then one of them climbed onto the back and pulled off the cover. All he found was sand.

Suddenly, a sandy hand shot out and threw the officer into the air. Sandman rose out of the back of the truck. The other officers started to shoot at him. They made holes in his body and grains of sand flew from the holes. But the gunshots didn't stop him.

And then, with a terrible cry, Sandman flew down the street like an angry sandstorm.

# Chapter 5
## The key and the kiss

The huge crowd of people were shouting and cheering for Spider-Man. Suddenly, someone called to Mary Jane.

'Hi, MJ!' She turned around and saw Harry Osborn. She had visited him in the hospital and he looked so much better now.

'Where's Pete?' Harry asked as he looked around.

'Taking photos, I guess,' she said.

In the past only two people knew Peter was Spider-Man – Mary Jane and Harry. But now only MJ knew Peter's secret and she wanted to keep it.

Harry asked why she wasn't at the theatre. She looked into his smiling face – at last someone had time to listen to her. She told him everything. He said he was really sorry.

'You look so good, Harry,' MJ said after a moment.

Harry smiled. 'A knock on the head and you're as free as bird.'

MJ replied, 'Knock me on the head then, please!'

They laughed together. For the first time that day she stopped thinking about her problems. Harry was just what she needed.

Gwen Stacy looked out nervously at the huge crowd in the square. She had never spoken in front of so many people before. She was nervous too because Spider-Man was out there.

She stepped up to the microphone and started to speak. She told the crowd about Spider-Man and how he saved her life. Everyone cheered loudly. A band started to play. And suddenly there he was! Spider-Man swung over the crowd. The crowd went crazy.

Slowly, upside-down, Spider-Man lowered himself to face Gwen.

She reached out and pulled down his mask to show his mouth. Gwen gave Spider-Man the key and then kissed him. It was a long, slow kiss. 'I just want to thank you for saving me,' said Gwen. The crowd went wild.

But one person in the crowd wasn't cheering – Mary Jane. Her first kiss with Spider-Man was exactly like this. Her eyes filled with tears and all the horrible feelings returned. Not even Harry could help her now.

A huge sandstorm was blowing through the streets. It was heading for the square. Suddenly, it blew through the crowd. Everyone ran to escape the angry winds. The cloud of sand raced round a corner and then disappeared …

Peter's spider sense woke up. A moment later the sandstorm shot down from the sky. WHOOOSH! It blew an armoured truck round and round like a leaf in the wind. The truck was taking lots of money and gold to a bank. Then the storm winds tore the top off the vehicle – Sandman had arrived!

The guard in the front of the truck turned and shot Sandman in the face. Sandman cried out in pain and then disappeared. But a moment later he rose up from the back of the truck and crashed down on the driver and the guard. Under the weight of the sand the two men could hardly breathe. The driver's foot pressed down hard and the vehicle shot down the street at high speed.

Spider-Man landed silently in the back of the truck. He stood next to Sandman who was normal size now. He looked more like the old Flint Marko. Spider-Man looked him in the eyes, but Marko wasn't afraid. Marko knew he had special powers, too. Then Spider-Man hit him hard, but his hand went straight through Sandman's body.

Suddenly, Sandman's hand began to grow. Soon it was huge. He used it to hit Spider-Man with all his power. Spider-Man and Sandman flew out of the truck, tearing off the back doors.

Spider-Man landed on one of the doors. He shot a line of

webbing at the truck and it pulled him along like a surfer. There was a lot of traffic on the road. Spider-Man had to move quickly to avoid the cars racing towards him.

Then he realised that the truck was heading straight towards a wall. He had to do something to save the men in the truck – and fast! He pulled himself along the webbing to the front of the truck. He made a web around the two men and threw them out of the truck. Then he shot another web for them to land in. Spider-Man was still in the truck and there was no time for him to get out …

CRASH! The truck crashed at top speed into the wall.

At first nothing moved. Smoke was rising from the pile of metal. But then, very slowly, Spider-Man pulled himself out. He was in a lot of pain but he wasn't seriously hurt. He was Spider-Man, after all!

The next day the *Daily Bugle* printed a story about Sandman on the front page. In big letters, it said, 'SANDMAN! EVEN SPIDER-MAN CAN'T STOP HIM!' There was also a personal note to Spider-Man from Jonah Jameson: 'GIVE BACK THE KEY!'

Peter shook his head and put down the paper. The story didn't even say that Spider-Man rescued the guards. And worst of all, the photo of Sandman was by Eddie Brock.

'Don't think about it,' Peter told himself. Tonight was his big night. He had more important things than Sandman to think about. Things like Mary Jane …

He put his hand in his pocket and pulled out the diamond ring. Still there. Still safe.

He took a deep breath, put the ring back in his pocket and left the room. He didn't see the sticky black goo moving across the wall towards his clothes cupboard.

# Chapter 6
## A painful evening

'Wow!' Peter thought as he walked into the Constellation Restaurant. It was the most expensive restaurant he had ever been to. New Yorkers in designer clothes talked and laughed over plates of amazing food. Peter gave his name to the head waiter. The waiter gave him an unfriendly look and replied sharply in French. Then, nervously, Peter took out the diamond ring.

'There's something I want to ask you …' he said.

Immediately the waiter's face changed. He smiled warmly at Peter. 'Maybe we can put the ring in the bottom of her glass?' he suggested. Peter nodded excitedly.

'And perhaps the musicians could play this …' Peter gave the waiter a piece of paper with the name of a song. The waiter said, 'Ah, yes! Their favourite.'

Peter sat alone waiting for Mary Jane. He practised the words he wanted to say. Then she appeared and came to the table. She looked extremely unhappy. She had just taken a new job – as a singing waitress in a club. The

club wasn't very nice but she needed the money. She looked around the restaurant without much interest.

'Isn't this place too expensive for you?' she asked.

'It's a special night,' Peter replied brightly. 'You're on Broadway. You're a star.'

MJ looked down at the table. She wanted to tell

Peter the truth but it was just too painful. 'I don't feel much like a star tonight,' she said sadly.

'You are a star. You've earned it,' Peter said warmly. He thought MJ was still worrying about the bad review.

He had more to say, but at that moment Gwen Stacy appeared at their table to say hello. She was at the restaurant with her parents. Her father, Captain Stacy, was very important in the New York police. 'It's so nice to meet you,' she said to MJ with a happy smile. 'Pete talks about you all the time.'

Mary Jane remembered Gwen from the day Spider-Man received the key. She hadn't realised that Spider-Man was kissing a girl he knew!

Peter looked uncomfortable. 'Gwen's my, er, study partner,' he said, 'in Dr Connors' class.'

Gwen asked Peter if he had a photo of Spider-Man kissing her. She'd love a photo of that! 'Who gets kissed by Spider-Man these days?' she joked.

MJ looked angrily at Peter. Gwen realised that she should go. 'I'll leave you two alone,' she said. She waved as she returned to her table. Peter waved back. The head waiter saw the wave and thought it was time to bring the champagne.

Mary Jane looked Peter in the eyes.

'Let me ask you something,' she said. 'When you kissed her … who was kissing her? Spider-Man or Peter?'

'What do you mean?' asked Peter.

'That was our kiss,' she said almost crying. 'Why would you do that?'

The truth was that Peter didn't know what to say. He didn't know why he kissed Gwen.

Mary Jane fought back the tears. 'He's not going to say sorry,' she realised.

'It doesn't matter,' she said finally. 'I don't feel very well.

I have to go.'

She got up and walked out of the restaurant. As she left, a violin player came towards the table. He was playing their song, 'Falling in Love'. Then the head waiter arrived with two glasses of champagne. Peter picked up Mary Jane's glass and took out the ring.

'I'll remember this moment for the rest of my life,' he thought, 'for all the wrong reasons.'

Peter stood next to the phone outside his room. He had just left a message for Mary Jane. He really needed to speak to her.

'Why didn't I say sorry?' he wondered. 'Why am I so stupid?' And then the phone rang. Peter answered it immediately. But it wasn't Mary Jane.

'Mr Parker, this is Captain Stacy,' said a man's voice. 'We've got some new information about the murder of your uncle, Ben Parker.'

Peter didn't understand. Uncle Ben's killer was caught long ago. What new information could they possibly have?

'Please come down to the police station immediately.'

Aunt May sat as still as a stone in the chair next to Peter's. 'We used to think that this man, Dennis Caradine, was the killer,' said Captain Stacy. He held up a photo. Peter knew the face well. Peter had allowed him to escape from a fight club with the night's money. He had chased him when he drove off in Uncle Ben's car after the murder. Captain Stacy put the photo down on his desk. 'We were wrong.'

Peter's heart stopped. 'Wrong? How could they be wrong?' he thought.

'The real killer is still free,' Captain Stacy explained and held up another photo. 'He's a thief who's been in and out of prison.'

Peter looked at the photo in disbelief. It was the man Spider-Man fought in the armoured truck.

'Two days ago, he escaped from prison,' Captain Stacy continued. 'He told another prisoner about the murder.'

Peter could hardly breathe. Peter had chased Dennis Caradine and he had died because of a terrible mistake. Peter felt so angry. It was too much. He ran straight out of the station. He couldn't look at Captain Stacy or think about Dennis Caradine for another moment.

# Chapter 7
## A new Spider-Man

Someone was knocking very softly on Peter's door. Peter got up slowly and opened the door. Mary Jane was standing there. He wasn't pleased to see her; he was too upset about Uncle Ben's killer.

'Aunt May called me,' she said. 'She told me about this criminal who killed Uncle Ben. She's worried about you.'

Peter couldn't speak. He turned and went back into the room. MJ followed him and closed the door. Her heart ached for Peter.

'You killed the wrong man,' she said. 'But you didn't know that when you pushed him …'

'I didn't kill him! I didn't push him,' Peter replied sharply. 'He was pointing a gun at me. I moved. He fell.'

MJ had chosen the wrong words, but she really wanted to help Peter. She didn't want to make things worse. 'If I can help you in some way, I'm here …' she said.

'Thank you for coming,' Peter answered, but his voice sounded flat and cold. He opened the door for Mary Jane. Right now he needed to be alone. He had to think about how to make things right.

'Everybody needs help sometimes,' she said as she walked out. 'Even Spider-Man.'

Peter didn't even say goodbye. He switched on his police radio. 'Uncle Ben's killer is out there …' he thought. 'Lots of other criminals are out there, too.'

He thought about Sandman and how he had escaped from Spider-Man. 'That won't happen again,' he promised himself. 'Criminals can escape from the cops, but they won't escape from Spider-Man. Not any more!'

Later that night Peter was lying on his bed wearing his Spider-Man suit. The police radio was still on, but Peter wasn't listening. He was in a deep sleep. The black goo moved from his clothes cupboard towards his bed. As it moved closer and closer, Peter's dreams became darker. He saw Flint Marko shoot Uncle Ben and Dennis Caradine fall to his death … over and over again.

The black goo moved slowly across Peter's red and blue suit until it covered it completely. It became part of Spider-Man's suit.

Peter opened his eyes. He was high up in the air above the city. He looked up and saw that he was hanging on a line of webbing from one of the tallest buildings.

'What's happening?' Peter asked in surprise.

Just then, he saw himself in the mirrored wall of the building.

'Wow!' he thought. 'Awesome!' His spider suit was completely black. And he felt really strong – much stronger than usual.

He ran straight down the side of the building. Then he jumped up high, turned in the air and landed on a very narrow wall. It was an impossible jump. 'I couldn't do that before!' thought Peter. He felt amazing. With this new black suit he could do anything.

'This feels good!' he said. 'This is something else!'

# Chapter 8
## Washed away

The next morning there was an urgent report on Peter's police radio. Someone was robbing a bank and Spider-Man had to act fast. Peter knew this was the work of Flint Marko. 'He's not going to escape this time,' thought Peter. He put on the new black suit and raced to the bank.

But Spider-Man arrived at the bank seconds too late. He saw Sandman escaping into the New York subway*.

Spider-Man was about to jump down after Sandman when Eddie Brock appeared.

'Love the new suit!' Eddie said as he took Spider-Man's photo.

Spider-Man was angry. The last thing he needed right now was Eddie Brock. He shot a line of webbing at the camera and pulled it from Eddie's hands. Then he jumped down into the subway tunnel after Sandman. Eddie couldn't believe it – Spider-Man wasn't such a good guy after all! And then he had an idea. He took out a second camera from his pocket. Quickly he took some pictures of the bank before the police arrived.

Spider-Man moved silently through the dark subway tunnel. Suddenly, he heard a train coming towards him. He pressed his body against the tunnel wall. The train raced past like the wind. Then he turned a corner and saw Flint Marko with bags of money in his arms. Spider-Man moved. Marko turned quickly but he couldn't see anyone. Spider-Man's new black suit hid him in the darkness.

*\* New York's underground railway.*

SLAM! Out of nowhere Spider-Man hit Marko hard in the face. Marko flew backwards, dropping the bags of money.

He got up and his body turned into sand. He ran at Spider-Man. WHAM! They both went flying through the tunnel. Spider-Man moved quickly to avoid a speeding train. Sandman knocked Spider-Man backwards. Then Spider-Man fired a web at Sandman but it missed. Sandman threw himself at Spider-Man but his head hit a passing train. It cut away half of Sandman's head. He screamed in pain and fell to his knees. Spider-Man noticed that one of Sandman's hands had landed in a pool of water. His hand was disappearing! Spider-Man realised that the water had come from a huge pipe next to them. He pulled at the top of the pipe with his hands. The pipe broke open and water shot everywhere. Sandman gave a terrible cry as the water washed him away. Soon there was nothing left of Sandman. Flint Marko was gone and Spider-Man didn't feel bad about it – not even a little bit.

When Peter returned home later that day, he met Mr Ditkovich. Mr Ditkovich owned the building and lived on the floor below Peter. Mr Ditkovich wanted his money for the month and he was not happy.

Peter was always late with the money for his room. Usually Peter was polite to Mr Ditkovich, but not today.

'I would pay on time if you mended anything. Like the lock on my door!' he shouted. He had the suit on under his clothes; he felt really powerful.

He went angrily into his room. He saw himself in the mirror. He looked different – like a wild animal. 'It's the suit,' he realised. 'It's changing me … It's making me dangerous.'

He couldn't wear the suit any more. He must throw it away. 'But what if someone found it?' he thought. He saw a box in the corner of his room. He put the suit in the box and closed the top. 'I'll keep it,' he thought. 'But I'll never wear it again.'

Harry Osborn was painting a picture. He was really enjoying himself. He stopped for a moment and looked around the room. Suddenly, he heard his father's voice in his head. He looked at himself in the mirror.

And then memories poured back into Harry's mind. He saw his father's dead body. Spider-Man lying on a sofa. A hand taking off Spider-Man's mask. Peter Parker's face!

'Remember me?' shouted Norman Osborn.

'Yes, father,' Harry replied. 'I remember everything now.'

'Why haven't you killed Peter Parker?'

Harry felt sick. Peter was his best friend.

'I won't listen to you any more,' Harry shouted. 'Leave me alone!'

Peter went to see his teacher, Dr Connors. He had a small piece of the black goo in his hand. He was really worried about the new black suit and its dangerous power. At first Dr Connors wasn't very happy to stop his work. But he could see from Peter's face that this was important. And when Peter showed him the black goo, he was very interested. He promised to examine it as soon as possible.

Mary Jane was in Harry's kitchen. She had called to tell him about her new job and he had invited her over for lunch. They were having so much fun together that Mary Jane forgot all her problems. Harry loved being with her … They were laughing and dancing when more memories came back into his head. He had loved Mary Jane! And he still loved her … He moved closer to MJ and looked into her eyes. For a moment they kissed. But then she pulled away. She loved Harry as a friend. 'I could never love Harry the way I love Peter,' she thought.

'You're thinking about Peter, aren't you?' Harry said angrily.

MJ got up to leave. 'That's right,' thought Harry. 'Run back to Peter like you always do!'

And then all his memories came back. He was jealous of Peter ... he loved Mary Jane ... she loved Peter ... Peter was Spider-Man! Harry could hear his father laughing in his head. His father was right. Peter Parker was his enemy. He had stolen everything that Harry had ever loved. He thought of a plan. Mary Jane must break up with Peter. Nothing could hurt his enemy more than this!

Mary Jane ran home from Harry's place. She was about to open her front door when the New Goblin appeared from nowhere. His strong arms took hold of Mary Jane. She tried to scream but no sound came out. The New Goblin had her in his power.

# Chapter 9
## Revenge

Peter walked through the park to meet Mary Jane. He had brought her favourite flowers. When MJ called him, she had sounded very upset. 'I've only been thinking about myself,' Peter realised.

He held out the flowers to her. She looked at them and felt terrible. Peter had remembered her favourite flowers! It just made things harder.

'This isn't easy for me,' she began. 'I have to tell you the truth. We can't be together any more.'

'But I love you,' Peter said.

'I'm lonely,' she replied. 'You're not there for me.'

Peter's heart was breaking.

She had to make it final. 'There's someone else,' she added. 'There's nothing more to talk about.'

Peter's world was falling to pieces. He had to fight to keep her. He got down on one knee. He started to ask her to marry him. But MJ didn't listen. She turned away to hide her tears. 'Just leave me alone!' she cried. Then she ran out of the park leaving Peter alone with the flowers.

Harry Osborn was hiding behind some trees near the bridge. He saw everything.

'Bravo!' he called to Mary Jane as she left the park. She had done exactly what he wanted.

Peter lay on his bed feeling terrible. He couldn't stop thinking about Mary Jane. 'What happened?' he wondered. 'Why won't she talk to me?'

He knew he had done some bad things. He wasn't there for her when she needed him. It was wrong to kiss Gwen. And he wasn't grateful for her help about Uncle Ben. But these weren't reasons to break up. He wanted to help Mary Jane, but he didn't know how.

He turned over and saw the box. 'Don't touch the suit,' he thought. 'It's dangerous. It changes you.'

He looked again at the box. 'Well, maybe I want to be different … Things can't get much worse …'

He moved towards the box, lifted up the top and pulled out the suit.

'I'll just wear it for a little while,' he promised. 'Until I feel better.'

Later that day Peter walked through Manhattan like a new man. With the suit under his clothes, he felt fantastic. 'Nothing can stop me now,' he thought. But then he walked past a newspaper-seller. He noticed the front page of the *Daily Bugle*. It said: 'SPIDER-MAN: THIEF!' Under this there was a photo of Spider-Man robbing a bank! Peter looked closely at the photo. Immediately he realised that it was two different photos. It was a fake! Someone had put them together to make Spider-Man into a criminal. And the name under the photo was Eddie Brock!

Peter was very angry.

'Eddie wants that job so much,' Peter thought, 'he's happy to lie about Spider-Man. Well, he's not going to get away with this.'

And he raced down the street towards the *Daily Bugle* office.

Peter found Eddie at his new desk in his new office. There were a lot of people from the newspaper there. They were celebrating Eddie's new job.

'Your picture is a fake!' Peter shouted.

'Give me a break,' Eddie said with a smile.

Peter pushed Eddie powerfully against a wall.

'Peter, please,' Eddie said in surprise. 'If anyone finds out, no newspaper will give me a job.'

At that moment, Robbie Robertson appeared at Peter's side. He was Jonah Jameson's number two at the newspaper. He couldn't believe that Peter Parker was attacking Eddie Brock! Peter was so quiet and shy.

Peter let go of Eddie and gave a photo to Robbie. It was

the real photo, the one Eddie had used in his 'Spider-Man: Thief!' photo. Peter knew Eddie would lose his job. But Peter didn't care any more. He just smiled.

Peter went silently into the Osborn house. He was wearing the black suit under his clothes. He didn't mean to put it on but he couldn't stop himself. He needed to speak to Harry about Mary Jane.

'What took you so long?' said Harry's voice. But it wasn't Harry. It was the New Goblin.

'What?' Peter asked in surprise.

'I was there for her, Pete,' said Harry. 'And when she kissed me …'

Peter threw himself angrily at Harry. He shot webs at his old friend, but Harry cut through them easily. Then Peter held onto Harry's arms and they crashed through the long mirror on the wall. Behind this mirror was the Goblin's secret room. Peter ran at Harry and pushed him to the floor. He could easily kill him there and then …

'Are you going to kill me like you killed my father?' Harry cried.

'Your father tried to kill me,' Peter shouted in his face. Finally, Peter was able to tell Harry the truth and he was enjoying it. 'He wasn't proud of you!' he cried. 'He hated you.'

Harry reached for a bomb and threw it at Peter. But Peter was too quick and he shot the bomb back at Harry.

BOOM! The bomb blew up near Harry's face. He cried in pain. Then he saw himself in the broken mirror and he screamed.

Peter heard Harry's screams behind him. This time he didn't help Harry. He jumped out of the window and away into the night.

Peter was on the phone outside his room. Dr Connors was telling him about the black goo.

'Something very similar was found in a meteorite in the 1970s,' said Dr Connors. 'It's very old, it's alive and it can think!'

'It can *think*?' Peter couldn't believe it. His black suit was alive!

'It can even change the way people act,' Dr Connors continued.

Peter already knew that. He had done some terrible things when he was wearing the suit.

'Stay away from it,' Dr Connors said finally. 'It could be dangerous.'

Peter knew Dr Connors was right. He should stay away from the suit.

'I'm just not sure that I want to,' he thought.

In a water pipe below the city some grains of sand were coming together. The water raced through the pipe and out into a small river. The grains joined together to make a hand, then an arm, then a body. Very slowly the body rose out of the water – Sandman was alive!

# Chapter 10
## The Jazz Room

Peter was laughing as he walked into the Jazz Room with Gwen. He had asked her out on a date earlier that afternoon. Gwen was looking really beautiful and they'd had a wonderful dinner together.

Peter looked around the small, dark club. 'So this is where Mary Jane is working,' he thought. 'I'm not surprised she's feeling so down.'

They found a table near the band. One of the musicians stepped up to the microphone and said, 'Let's hear from you, Mary Jane!'

MJ put down some drinks and hurried over to the band.

'Isn't that Mary Jane, your old girlfriend?' Gwen asked Peter in surprise.

Peter smiled and said, 'Crazy, huh?'

Just as MJ was about to sing, Peter jumped up and started to play the piano. Mary Jane stepped back from the microphone in surprise. Peter played the piano with amazing skill, then he jumped onto the dance floor. Under his clothes the black suit made him dance really well. He took Gwen in his arms, turned her around, then lowered her backwards. He was about to kiss Gwen when she suddenly pushed him away. 'This is for her, isn't it?' Gwen cried looking at Mary Jane. 'I'm so sorry,' she said to MJ and ran out of the club.

Peter watched her go. He didn't feel bad about using her. He had come here for revenge and now he had it.

The manager came over and asked Peter to leave. When Peter refused, he asked the doorman to throw him out. The doorman was huge, but Peter knocked him over easily. Then MJ tried to talk to Peter. She walked up behind him. Without looking he turned round and hit MJ. She fell to the floor.

Suddenly, everything stopped, nobody moved.

'What's happened to you?' MJ whispered.

'I don't know,' Peter answered, feeling sick.

But he knew it was the suit. He had it on again under his clothes. The suit was changing him into a bad guy – a really bad guy.

Peter ran out of the Jazz Room and through the city streets. He didn't know where he was going. He ran until he saw an old church. He stopped and looked up at the beautiful broken windows. He needed somewhere to think. He wanted to get high above the noise of the city.

He ran into the church and up the stairs to the highest point. He took off his shirt and climbed outside. He looked out over the city in his black suit. Then he swung down into the bell room.

'I have to destroy the suit,' he thought. He tried to pull it off, but it stuck to his skin. It had become a part of him. For a moment Peter was pleased – he didn't really want to give it up. He enjoyed feeling powerful and dangerous! But then he thought of Mary Jane. She had looked so hurt in the club. His heart ached for her. No, he had to destroy it!

He tore at the suit with his fingers and screamed in pain. But it wouldn't come off. Then he fell back into one of the bells. CLANG! At the sound of the bell, the black goo started to come off. Bits dropped from his body onto the broken floor. CLANG! He rang another bell and more fell from his skin. It dropped through to the floor below. Someone was standing there, watching this amazing sight. Eddie Brock!

'Peter Parker is Spider-Man!' Eddie couldn't believe it. 'The two people who destroyed my life are really one!'

This explained everything. Peter was the only person before Eddie to take photos of Spider-Man. And now he understood why Peter felt so angry about the fake photo.

Eddie had of course lost his job because of that photo. His life fell to pieces on that day. Gwen didn't want to see him any more. He had lost everything. He had gone to the church to ask God for something. He wanted to ask for … revenge!

As Peter fought with the suit, bits of it fell onto Eddie. Peter had no idea that Eddie was there. The black goo landed on Eddie's hands, his face and his tongue. A bright white light shot through Eddie's body. He felt like he was on fire. He smiled crazily as Spider-Man's powers raced through his body. He became a terrible new enemy for Spider-Man. He was Venom!

Peter was in the shower. He was washing away the last bits of the black goo from his body. For the first time in weeks he felt clean.

A little later there was a knock on Peter's door. It was Aunt May. She was very worried about him.

'How's MJ?' she asked.

Peter shook his head. 'I don't know. I haven't heard from her.'

'Did you ask her to marry you?'

'No,' he answered. 'You were right. I'm not ready.'

'But you seemed so sure.'

Peter took out the diamond ring and gave it back to Aunt May.

'I hurt MJ,' he said. 'I don't know what to do …'

'Forgive yourself, Peter,' she answered. 'I believe in you. Find a way to make this right.'

And she put the ring back in Peter's hand.

It was late at night and Flint Marko stood in the street below his daughter's room. He missed her so much.

Just then Flint saw a man in black. He was watching him in the darkness.

'Do I know you?' Flint shouted.

'I'm the enemy of your enemy,' Venom replied.

Flint didn't understand. Eddie explained that they both hated Spider-Man. Together they could destroy him.

'I just want him off my back,' Flint agreed.

Eddie smiled. Sandman was the perfect partner.

He put his arm around Flint's shoulder.

'Follow me,' he said.

# Chapter 11
## Partners in crime

All around the city people watched TV screens. A taxi was hanging high above the city of New York in a huge black web! There was a young woman inside. The TV news reporter said she was an actress called Mary Jane Watson.

Venom wrote a message in the web: 'SPIDER-MAN – STOP US IF YOU CAN.'

Peter was watching, too. This time he really needed help. But who in the world could help Spider-Man?

Harry sat in a dark room watching the action on TV. His face would get better, but he would never look normal. He was feeling very angry with Peter and very sorry for himself.

Peter entered the room silently through a window.

'Harry, I can't take them both,' Peter said softly. 'She needs us.'

'If you want to save MJ, you'll have to do it yourself,' Harry shouted. 'Get out!'

Peter knew Harry would never forgive him.

But after Peter left, Bernard came down the stairs. Bernard had seen and heard many things during his years at the Osborn house.

'Harry,' he said. 'There's something I have to tell you. I saw your father the night he died. I cleaned his injury. I know your father's death was his own fault.'

Mary Jane was angry and afraid. Once again she was in terrible danger because of Spider-Man. Suddenly, she screamed as part of the web broke and the taxi almost crashed to the ground. There was a huge truck in the web above her. The truck was full of concrete blocks.

And then Spider-Man arrived. He swung down and landed on the front of the taxi.

At that moment MJ forgot all her angry feelings. Finally Spider-Man was there for her. Venom swung towards them and kicked Spider-Man through the front window. Glass flew everywhere. Venom climbed into the taxi. The black goo on his face was moving all the time. Spider-Man could see Eddie's face and realised what had happened. The black goo had found a new partner in crime!

Venom hit Spider-Man in the face and they both fell out of the taxi. They landed on one of the floors of an unfinished office building. Venom jumped onto Spider-Man and the two enemies were face to face. Venom smiled a horrible smile. Soon he would have his revenge …

At that moment the truck above MJ started to move. Some of the concrete blocks fell into the taxi. MJ managed to push one of the blocks out of the taxi and down onto Venom below. Spider-Man broke away from his enemy but

Venom shot webbing at Spider-Man. The webbing flew around Spider-Man's neck and tied him to a metal post.

Suddenly, the truck above MJ broke away. It hit the taxi as it fell. MJ managed to jump out into Venom's huge web.

In the street below Sandman was ready to join the fight. All the grains of his body came together and a huge mountain of sand raced towards Spider-Man. Was this the end for Spider-Man?

BOOM! Suddenly, a bomb hit Sandman and blew away his head. Harry had arrived! He flew down to Spider-Man and took his hand. Together the two old friends flew on the Sky-Stick and faced their enemies. Harry shot bombs at Sandman while Spider-Man attacked Venom. But then Venom knocked Harry and Spider-Man off the Sky-Stick. He picked up a metal pipe and pointed it at Spider-Man. One end of the pipe was very sharp.

'Don't give in to the suit,' Spider-Man shouted at Venom. 'It changes you … It makes you bad!'

Venom smiled a horrible smile. 'I like being bad,' he said. 'It makes me happy.'

Harry threw a bomb at Venom. He fell back but got up again and ran at Spider-Man with two sharp metal pipes.

This time Spider-Man would die! Suddenly, Harry jumped in front of Venom and the two metal pipes shot deep into his stomach. Harry fell screaming to the floor below.

Quickly, Spider-Man drove some metal pipes into the floor around Venom. They made a circle all around him. He was caught like an animal. Spider-Man ran round the outside of the circle, hitting each pipe with a piece of metal. CLANG! CLANG! The sound of metal on metal! The black goo started to move and fall from Venom's body. Spider-Man pulled Eddie out of the goo, but Eddie didn't want to be saved. He jumped back just as Spider-Man threw a bomb at the goo. BOOM! There was fire and smoke, then Eddie Brock and the goo were gone.

Suddenly, Flint Marko appeared at Peter's side. He needed to tell Peter about Uncle Ben's death. He explained that his daughter was dying. She was all he had in the world. He needed money and he was frightened. Uncle Ben had told him, 'Put down the gun and go home.' He realised now that Uncle Ben was trying to help him. But a moment later, his partner, Dennis Caradine had run up with the money. They had to escape. In the heat of the moment he shot Uncle Ben.

'I did a terrible thing. I've wanted to go back and change it so many times,' said Marko. 'If you can't forgive me, I understand.'

Peter thought for a moment. 'I've done some terrible things too,' he said. He looked Flint Marko in the eyes. He knew Marko was telling the truth.

'I forgive you,' said Peter.

Then Flint Marko disappeared in a cloud of sand.

Down on the floor below, MJ sat beside Harry. Peter raced down to join them. Was he already too late?

'How are you, Harry?' Peter asked.

'I've been better,' Harry replied with a weak smile.

'We'll get through this,' said Peter, but he could see his friend was dying. 'I was wrong to hurt you. I was wrong to say those things.'

'None of that matters, Peter,' Harry said softly. 'You're my friend – my best friend.'

And with these final words Harry Osborn died.

## Epilogue
## The songbird

Peter could hear Mary Jane's lovely voice as he walked towards the Jazz Room. He stopped at the entrance. There was a large photo of Mary Jane next to a wonderful review. Peter read the words and smiled: 'DON'T MISS HER! A BEAUTIFUL SONGBIRD HAS FLOWN INTO TOWN.'

He pulled open the door and went into the club. Mary Jane smiled at Peter as he walked into the room. He waited until she had finished her song. Then he took her to the dance floor. The band started to play 'Falling in Love'.

Peter looked into MJ's eyes. 'We have a lot to talk about,' he said.

MJ put a finger to his lips. 'Let's not talk about us,' she told him. 'Just shut up and dance.'

And so they danced.

## FACT FILE

# Spider-Man 3

*Spider-Man 3* came out in cinemas in May 2007. It continues the story of Peter Parker and tells of Spider-Man's fight against some exciting new villains. We asked some questions about this amazing film …

Sam Raimi, the director

### So, a third Spider-Man film! Did the same team work on it?

Director Sam Raimi came back for the third time to work with same acting team of Tobey Maguire (Peter Parker / Spider-Man), Kirsten Dunst (Mary Jane Watson) and James Franco (Harry Osborn).

### How did they choose the villains for *Spider-Man 3*?

Venom is really popular with Spider-Man fans so he had to be in it! Sam Raimi and Tobey Maguire both love Sandman and wanted him in the film. He's an unusual villain. He doesn't want to rule the world. He just wants to help his sick daughter.

### And Harry Osborn is the New Goblin?

He is, but he's not very good at being a villain. He has too many difficult feelings. He wants revenge for his father's death, but he still loves his old friend Peter. And he still loves Mary Jane. He's not a strong character like his father, so he can't be a strong villain.

# The Film

### Is Peter any different in this story?

Peter is still 'just an average guy', as Spider-Man creator Stan Lee calls him. But he's really tested this time. There are questions about his feelings and his mind. 'Peter has to deal with his dark side,' said Avi Arad, one of the film's producers.

### Why is the colour black important in this film?

Some black goo arrives on earth in a meteorite. It takes over Peter's suit. When Peter wears the black suit, he's different. His darker feelings are stronger as well as his powers.

### Anything to look out for in the film?

Stan Lee has small parts in all the Spider-Man films. This time he has a speaking part and talks to Peter Parker.

## Film Launch

New York City loves Spider-Man! *Spider-Man 3* was launched in Manhattan with a whole Spider-Man week. They had special events at the Natural History Museum, the city gardens and the zoo.

---

**How would you launch a Spider-Man film in your town? What events would you organise?**

---

### Does *Spider-Man 3* have new music?

Yeah, Yeah, Yeahs

Spider-Man has the same tune as in the earlier films. There are new tunes for the new villains – Venom and Sandman. The film also has songs by Snow Patrol and Yeah Yeah Yeahs (above).

---

**What do these words mean? You can use a dictionary.**

villain    average    mind    to deal with    launch    event

**FACT FILE**

# SPIDER-MAN'S

Spider-Man protects ordinary New Yorkers against ordinary criminals. But sometimes he has to face some super-criminals. Here are three of the best from the Spider-Man films …

## The Green Goblin

aka: **Norman Osborn**  Film: *Spider-Man*

**Who is he?** Norman Osborn runs a big scientific company called OsCorp. They have made a special gas for the army. It makes people stronger and more intelligent.

**How does he change?** Norman tests the gas but it goes wrong. He becomes stronger and cleverer, but also crazy. He changes into the Green Goblin!

**Powers:** He's stronger, faster and cleverer than a man.

Who is Spider-Man's most dangerous enemy?
Who is your favourite?

# ENEMIES

## Doc Ock

aka: **Dr Otto Octavius** Film: *Spider-Man 2*

**Who is he?** Dr Otto Octavius is a brilliant scientist. He has designed a machine that makes cheap energy. He uses four metal arms to control the machine.

**How does he change?** The energy machine goes wrong and the metal arms take control of Dr Otto Octavius. He becomes Doc Ock.

**Powers:** He's much stronger than a man. He can walk up walls and jump from building to building.

> **Which of these super powers would you like?**
> **wall-climbing**
> **sky-boarding**
> **web-shooting**
> **a spider sense**

## Venom

aka: **Eddie Brock** Film: *Spider-Man 3*

**Who is he?** Like Peter, he's a photographer for the *Daily Bugle*.

**How does he change?** Eddie is watching when Spider-Man tries to destroy the black suit. Some of the black goo from the suit falls onto Eddie. It sticks to Eddie's body and turns him into Venom.

**Powers:** The black goo gives Eddie the same powers as Spider-Man. Peter can't feel him with his spider sense.

> **What do these words mean? You can use a dictionary.**
> **aka (also known as)   army   glider   energy**

**FACT FILE**

# BROADWAY
## The Street of Dreams

*"Tonight was Mary Jane's opening night on Broadway. Peter was so proud that his girlfriend was the star of the show."*

**Broadway is one of the most famous streets in New York. It is also the most famous theatre area in the world. Many young actors dream of starring in one of its shows.**

## Did you know ...?

- There are 39 Broadway theatres (these are theatres with more than 500 seats). Most of them were built between 1910 and 1930
- Off-Broadway describes smaller theatres with between 100 and 499 seats.
- Some of these theatres are on Broadway; others are in streets around Broadway.

- The longest running Broadway show is 'The Phantom of the Opera', a musical which opened in January 1988.

- The longest running Off-Broadway show is 'The Fantasticks', a play at the very small Sullivan Street Playhouse. It started in May 1960 and continues today.

- You can buy tickets for Broadway shows from the famous TKTS (tickets) box. People queue for half-price tickets from early each morning.

> Which do you prefer – plays, musicals or films? How are they different?

## That's show business!

When a new Broadway show opens, the producer doesn't know when it will close. Success depends on three things:
- what the reviews say
- what people tell their friends
- good advertising

Mary Jane loses her job in 'Manhattan Memories' because of bad reviews. If people hear that the star is no good, the show will flop. So the producer changes the star. It's hard, but that's show business!

## The Great White Way

Broadway started as a Native American trail called the Wickquasgeck Trail. It went across Manhattan Island from north to south. When the Dutch came to this area, they used the trail and made it into a road. They called it *Breede weg* - the 'broad' (meaning 'wide') way. The British renamed it Broadway.

In 1880 Broadway became the first street in the USA to have electric street lights. In 1902 a newspaper called it the Great White Way because of all the lights along it. Some people still call it this name today.

> **What do these words mean?**
> **You can use a dictionary.**
> musical   advertising   flop
> Native American   trail

# SELF-STUDY ACTIVITIES

# Chapters 1-4

**Before you read**

*Use a dictionary for this section.*

**1** Choose the right word.

**bomb crane fake goo grain mask spider**

a) It's thick and sticky.
b) It covers a person's face.
c) It's very, very small.
d) It's a very tall machine.
e) It has eight legs.
f) It can kill people.
g) It isn't real.

**2** Complete the sentences with the correct form of these words.

**breathe cheer memory responsibility review swing**

a) She can't remember anything. She's lost her … .
b) The newspaper gave the show a very bad … .
c) The crowd … very loudly when their team won.
d) Looking after young children is a big … .
e) They went outside and … in the fresh air.
f) The animal … through the trees and then jumped down.

**3** Look at People and Places on pages 4-5. Answer these questions.

a) Who is New York City's own hero?
b) Who lives alone because her husband is dead?
c) Who wants revenge on Peter for his father's death?
d) Who sometimes works as a model?
e) Which two photographers work for the Daily Bugle?
f) Which of Spider-Man's enemies has the same powers as him?

**After you read**

**4** Are these sentences right or wrong?

a) Harry isn't at the theatre.
b) Peter and MJ don't see the meteorite when it lands.
c) Penny Marko is angry with her father.
d) Aunt May thinks Peter needs a better job.
e) Harry thinks Spider-Man killed his father.
f) The New Goblin dies after attacking Peter.

**5** Answer the questions.
  **a)** How does Flint Marko become Sandman?
  **b)** Why is MJ angry with Peter after she gets a bad review?
  **c)** Why does Eddie make Gwen feel uncomfortable?
  **d)** What does Jonah Jameson really want?
  **e)** Why is Peter happy about Harry's memory loss?
  **f)** Why doesn't MJ tell Peter that she has lost her job?

# Chapters 5-8

## Before you read
  **6** What do you think?
  **a)** What is Sandman going to do next?
  **b)** Will Harry's memory return?

## After you read
  **7** Who says these things? Who are they speaking to?
  **a)** 'A knock on the head and you're as free as a bird.'
  **b)** 'I just want to thank you for saving me.'
  **c)** 'Give back the key!'
  **d)** 'You're on Broadway. You're a star.'
  **e)** 'That was our kiss.'
  **f)** 'We were wrong.'

  **8** Put these sentences in order.
  **a)** Spider-Man washes Sandman completely away.
  **b)** MJ goes to see Peter, but he doesn't want her help.
  **c)** Spider-Man wakes up wearing his new black suit.
  **d)** Harry and MJ have lunch and lots of fun together.
  **e)** The black goo becomes part of Spider-Man's suit.
  **f)** Eddie Brock takes some pictures of the bank.
  **g)** The New Goblin attacks Mary Jane.
  **h)** Spider-Man and Sandman fight in the subway.
  **i)** Peter puts the new black suit away in a box.

# SELF-STUDY ACTIVITIES

**9** What do you think?
    **a)** Is it the end for Sandman?
    **b)** Will MJ break up with Peter?
    **c)** Will Peter be able to give up the suit?

## Chapters 9-Epilogue

**Before you read**

**10** What do you think? Write your feelings about these people.
    **a)** Peter
    **b)** MJ
    **c)** Harry
    **d)** Eddie Brock

**After you read**

**11** Where do these things happen?
    **a)** MJ breaks up with Peter.
    **b)** Peter attacks Eddie Brock.
    **c)** Peter and Harry fight.
    **d)** Peter dances with Gwen.
    **e)** Eddie Brock becomes Venom.

**12** Answer the questions.
    **a)** Why do Venom and Sandman put MJ in danger?
    **b)** At first Harry doesn't want to help Peter. Why?
    **c)** Why does Harry change his mind?
    **d)** Why does MJ forget her angry feelings?
    **e)** Venom doesn't want to give up the suit. Why?
    **f)** Why does Flint Marko want to speak to Peter?
    **g)** Does Harry forgive Peter in the end?

**13** What do you think?
    **a)** What will happen to Flint Marko?
    **b)** What does Peter want to talk to MJ about?